Chubby Cheeks

& The Brighter Side of Black

Written and Illustrated by
Roland G. Davis

AuthorHouse™
1663 Liberty Drive
Bloomington, IN 47403
www.authorhouse.com
Phone: 833-262-8899

Because of the dynamic nature of the Internet, any web addresses or links contained in this book may have changed
since publication and may no longer be valid. The views expressed in this work are solely those of the author and do
not necessarily reflect the views of the publisher, and the publisher hereby disclaims any responsibility for them.

Any people depicted in stock imagery provided by Getty Images are models,
and such images are being used for illustrative purposes only.
Certain stock imagery © Getty Images.

This book is printed on acid-free paper.

ISBN: 978-1-4490-2674-5 (sc)

Library of Congress Control Number: 2009910982

Print information available on the last page.

Published by AuthorHouse 08/12/2024

From Genesis:

In the beginning the Earth was without form and void.
The Heavens were as pitch & *Blackness* was upon the face of the deep.
The spirit of the Lord moved upon the face of the waters and proclaimed…

"Let there be light!"

Dawn in the city, Any-town, U.S.A.

The Sun graced the Heaven's in a spectacular way.

Bursting from the East, it tainted the sky gold and red.

I stretched once, maybe twice, then jumped out of my bed.

I went out on the porch to take in this grand view

and ponder on what, today, I could do.

As I stood on the deck, I began to breathe deep.

The air filled my lungs, boy it sure tasted sweet!

"MMMMMMMMMM... AAAAAAAHHHHHH!!"

My first Saturday off... and it's been a few weeks

since I really spent time with my son, 'Chubby Cheeks'.

We decided to spend this day out hard at play

so we packed a big lunch then went off on our way.

We shot 'Hoops' at the playground.

'Chubby' beat me 12 - 2.

We built a kite on the golf course.

'Chubby' cheered when it flew.

We toured the city.

How strange, I've lived here all my life

yet I never found time to take in all the sights.

'Chubby Cheeks' being younger,

and in much better health,

ran all through the city; taking in all its wealth.

I was "fading fast", though I tried not to show.

'Chubby Cheeks' said, *"Hurry Daddy!*
Boy, old men sure are slow".

"Watch your mouth, boy!" I scolded,

in my most playful voice.

And I kept up with 'Chubby', though I had no real choice.

We went down to the river and strolled the bike path.

In the air was the faint scent of freshly cut grass.

"What about that spot Daddy, by that tree on the hill?

We can eat our lunch there; it's a great spot to 'chill'."

So we sat under the shade of a deciduous tree,

on a hill eating lunch, just 'Chubby' and me.

We had tuna on whole wheat with chips on the side.

For dessert we ate grapes, the red seedless kind.

As we sat there and dined, the sky grew very Black.

Suddenly lightning flashed and thunder did crack.

A bell started to ring deep inside of my brain

and I remembered, the weatherman said it would rain.

Quickly, we packed up our picnic and ran down to the street.

We jumped into the car... the rain cam down in 'sheets'.

"Well we made it, my son, and with no time to spare!"

But as I spoke I noticed something strange in the air.

'Chubby Cheeks' mood had altered

just like 'Jekyll and Hyde', so I asked,

"Chubby, tell me, what ails you inside?!"

'Chubby' turned slowly to face me,

and with eyes somewhat sad he asked,

"Daddy, how come only Black *things are bad?"*

"Only Black *things are bad?! Son, I don't understand.*

Could you please explain what made you ask that, young man?"

"Well I'm sure that you've noticed," 'Chubby' said with a pout.

"If you faint or 'keel over', that's known as a Blackout.*"*

"My son, you're so clever. What an excellent pun."

'Chubby Cheeks' said, *"Thanks Daddy but I wasn't quite done."*

He continued to speak keeping with the same text,

and this is what my son had to say next:

"You are taking a stroll; a cat crosses your path...

Now you have bad luck because that kitty was **Black.**

If a man joins a club but can't fit in at all

the club members may vote to have that man **Blackballed.**

When a person is evil or bad from the start,

then that person is said to possess a **Blackheart.** *"*

'Chubby Cheek' went on listing, barely taking a breath…

"*There is* Black magic, Black plague *and even* Black death.

You can Black list *some* Blackguard *in your little* Black book,

then Blackmail *the* Black-hearted, Black market *crook.*

Or Blackjack *the* Black sheep *if he refuses to pay…*

then just like Black ice, *make a slick getaway.*

And as he poured out his heart, the sad fact it revealed,

was how small all these terms had made my son feel.

'Chubby' ended by saying,

"*… And we came out to play, now these* Black clouds

brought rain, which ruined our day."

Then he sat back and sighed…

I scratched my head.

There was truth and some anger

in what 'Chubby' had said.

Surely this day would end on a very bad note

if there wasn't as much truth in the words that I spoke.

"Son, our day isn't ruined and those **Black clouds** *do have worth.*

They only brought rain to nourish the Earth.

*As for "*Black *being bad" I don't think that's quite right.*

You see son it was **Black** *that gave birth to the light.*

Black has luster, it sparkles and does its best shining

when a **Black** *lump of coal is pressed into a diamond."*

Out in space there is **Black** *stretching way beyond Mars*

and if it wasn't for **Black,** *at night, you wouldn't see stars.*

*"***Black** *is a gift from the Lord; you might think that corn,*

but at sunrise on a Sunday, a **Black** *child was born.*

He had lovely brown eyes and small little feet

but most precious of all were his fat, chubby, cheeks."

'Chubby Cheeks' began smiling. In a strange sort of way,

it was almost as if he remembered that day.

His smile did not dim, as he extended his hands.

We embraced then 'Chubby Cheeks' kissed his 'ole man'.

I look at this sweet child and said, *"Why'd you do that?"*

"Because Daddy, you make me feel proud to be Black.*"*

I started the car and we headed for home.

"It's time we got back son, mother's there all alone."

Back at home on the sofa, by the fireplace,

'Chubby' listed more things that cast *Black* in good taste.

He then shortened the list, choosing quality instead.

Then he came up to my study soon after and said;

"You know Black boards *aid teachers, Dad."*

"…Is that a fact?"

"... And accountants keep businessmen's funds 'In-the-Black'.

Some T.V. show 'Hillbillies' *struck it rich with* Black gold,

and 'Black Beauty', *by far, is the best story told."*

"Is that 'bout the horse who won many a race?"

"Yes, but I also see Black beauty *when I look on mom's face."*

At that exact moment, mother entered the room.

She blushed some then said, *"Dinner will be ready soon."*

Then she left quick as that but poked back in head.

She blew 'Chubby' a kiss then he turned beet red.

Later on while at dinner, 'Chubby Cheeks' said the grace,

he told Mom of our day as he cleaned off his plate.

"What an excellent meal, Mom!"

'Chubby Cheeks' and I said.

We ate cake, cleaned the dishes and then we all went to bed.

"Say your prayers, 'Chubby Cheeks',
and thank GOD up above for all he has given… oh,
and send him my love."

'Chubby Cheeks' bowed his head and noticed right away

that with his eyes closed real tight;

he saw Black when he prayed.

"All finished," said 'Chubby'.

Then, as he jumped in the sack he said,

"Daddy, the Lord sends his love back."

"Good night, 'Chubby'," I said,

taking his clothes from the floor.

I pulled down the shade, and then turned for the door…

"Hey, Daddy…"

"Yes, 'Chubby'?"

*"There's something I've noticed about the night.
Sometimes* Black *can be scary. Please leave on the hall light."*

"Good night."

Printed in the United States
by Baker & Taylor Publisher Services